To _____

● ●

From _____

ALL THINGS WISE AND WONDERFUL

A big little book of hints

© Pasadena Art Alliance 1975

The Pasadena Art Alliance is
an incorporated independent
organization, the purpose of
which is to support the Arts
in Southern California.

It is better to know some of
the questions than all of
the answers.

James Thurber

Table of contents

Around the house

●●●●●●●●●●●●●●●●●●●●●●●●●●●●●●●●●●●●

It is very important that before attacking <u>any stain</u> immediately soak up all excess liquid with layers of absorbent towels.

To <u>remove ink stain from rug</u>, drench the stained area with solution of half water and half white vinegar, taking care that ink does not splash nor spread. Do not rub, but absorb moisture with terry cloth. Part of

the ink will come out with
each application. Repeat.

●●●●●●●●●●●●●●●●●●●●●●●●●●

Stains from ball point pen
can be removed by sponging
area with sour milk or
vinegar and milk. Repeat.

Clean your fingers before
you point at my spots.

B. Franklin

Remove crayon marks from
painted wall with lighter
fluid.

●●●●●●●●●●●●●●●●●●●●●●●

Remove crayon marks from
linoleum with silver polish.

To remove stains from marble,
try a solution of peroxide
and a few drops of ammonia.
Allow to set for several
hours. Repeat if necessary.

<u>To clean marble</u>, dip quarter
of lemon in salt; rub; let
stand for a few minutes.
Wash off with soap and water.

●●●●●●●●●●●●●●●●●●●●●●●●●●●

<u>Polish marble</u> with chalk
moistened with water.

Life is made up of marble
and mud.

Nathaniel Hawthorne

To <u>remove grease stains</u>
<u>from rug</u>, brush baking soda
or cornmeal lightly through
the pile; allow to stand
overnight, then vacuum. On
synthetic rugs apply shellac
thinner or denatured alcohol
to the grease spot.

<u>To treat a combination
grease and non-grease stain</u>,
treat for non-grease first.
Go over soiled area with
a solution of cool water and
detergent; rinse thoroughly
and allow to dry. Now
sponge the grease stain with

cleaning fluid. If stain
persists, use mild bleach,
with caution!

Try a paste of lemon
juice and cornmeal on <u>grease</u>
<u>stains</u>.

The wheel that squeaks the loudest is the one that gets the grease.

Josh Billings

To <u>remove pet stains</u>
(urine) <u>from rug</u>, immediately apply solution of 1 oz. clear ammonia and 8 oz. cold water. Let stand until "bubbling" stops. Sponge with fresh water.

Douse <u>pet stains</u> on rug
with carbonated or quinine
water. Allow to dry.

<u>Pet stains</u> on rug respond
to sponging with solution
of white vinegar and cold
water.

There are three faithful
friends--an old wife, an
old dog and ready money.

B. Franklin

To <u>treat red wine stain</u>,
stretch soiled area of
tablecloth or napkin across
sink and pour boiling water
through the fabric from a
height of at least 2 or 3
feet; the more force, the

better. If stain persists,
scrub with naptha soap.

●●●●●●●●●●●●●●●●●●●●●●●

Boil stained portion of
fabric in milk before
laundering to <u>remove red
wine stain.</u>

It's a naive domestic
Burgundy without any
breeding, but I think
you'll be amused by its
presumption.

James Thurber

If <u>red wine</u> is spilled at
the table, cover stain at
once with coarse salt or
ordinary table salt.

●●●●●●●●●●●●●●●●●●●●●●●●●

Sponge <u>red wine stain</u> with
alcohol before laundering.

Saturate <u>wine stain on rug</u>
with carbonated water; cover
stain with towel. Stomp to
absorb moisture.

●●●●●●●●●●●●●●●●●●●●●●●●●

Try a few drops of glycer-
ine on <u>ball point pen stains</u>
before laundering.

In these days the greater part of whitewashing is done in ink.

G. D. Prentice

Soak <u>fruit stains</u> in
milk; then stretch
stained fabric over sink and
pour boiling water through
from a height. (See
"wine stains".)

<u>Fruit stains on table
linen</u> disappear if powdered starch is applied at
once and left on the stain
for a few hours before
laundering.

A rotten apple spoils

his companion.

                B. Franklin

To <u>treat peach stains</u>,
cover area with salt, let
stand for 24 hours; wash
in lukewarm water.

●●●●●●●●●●●●●●●●●●●●●●●●

Remove <u>lipstick stains</u>
from table napkins with
rubbing alcohol.

Saturate <u>lipstick stains</u> with small amount of salad oil. Launder at once.

● ●

<u>Paint stains</u> respond to scrubbing with a solution of half turpentine and half ammonia.

High heels were invented by
a woman who had been kissed
on the forehead.

Christopher Morley

To remove grass stains,
wash in naptha soap and
cold water.

●●●●●●●●●●●●●●●●●●●●●●●●●

To remove oil stains, try
applying paste of sugar and
water to spot on fabric
before laundering.

To <u>remove wax from table</u> <u>linen</u>, try placing facial tissue folded several times under and over the area and pressing with a warm iron.

●●●●●●●●●●●●●●●●●●●●●●●●

Remove <u>coffee and tea</u> <u>stains</u> with boiling water.

Dunking is bad taste but tastes good.

Robert Benchley

To remove _rust stains_ on
metal tools and utensils:
Try sticking knife blade in
raw onion; rub with cork
dipped in olive oil; rub
with typewriter eraser; rub
with lemon juice and salt.

To <u>treat rust stains</u> on white or colored fabrics, saturate stain with lime or lemon juice, cover with salt and set in the sun. Launder in the usual manner. Repeat if stain persists.

To <u>remove rust stains from white fabric</u>, make a paste of cream of tartar and hot water. Let stand for five minutes before laundering.

Sloth, like rust, consumes
faster than labor wears,
while the used key is
always bright.

R. W. Emerson

Soak <u>blood stains</u> first in cold water. After blood starts to fade, scrub with hot water and soap.

●●●●●●●●●●●●●●●●●●●●●●●●

To get <u>chewing gum</u> out of fabrics, use ice first, then cleaning fluid.

To <u>remove chocolate stains</u>,
sprinkle with powdered
borax, soak in cold water
for 20 minutes, then pour
boiling water through
fabric from a height.
(See "wine stains".)

Candy

Is dandy

But liquor

Is quicker.

Ogden Nash

Remove <u>white rings from wood</u>
surfaces by rubbing with:

1. Wood ash and raw potato;
2. Cigarette ash and licked
   finger;
3. Thin paste of wood ashes
   and salad oil;
4. Mayonnaise

Scratches on light wood

can be repaired by rubbing
with the meat of a walnut
or pecan.

●●●●●●●●●●●●●●●●●●●●●●●●

Camouflage scratches on
dark wood with iodine.

Scratch a lover, and find
a foe.

Dorothy Parker

<u>Scorch stains</u> are extremely difficult to remove. Avoid scorching by taking care that all soap has been completely rinsed from fabrics before ironing.

The following suggestions
for <u>removing scorch stains</u>
may work:

1. Sponge white shirts or
   linens with cotton soaked
   in peroxide;

2. Lightly brush scorch from
   silks or woolens;

3. Do not wet, but place
   article in sunshine;
4. Make paste of baking soda
   and water, place in sun;
5. Rub with lemon juice and
   place in sun.

If a man should suddenly be changed to a woman, he couldn't get his clothes off.

E. W. Howe

<u>Enemies of silver:</u>

Detergents, mustard, eggs;

Anything containing sulphur;

Rubber, including rubber
   bands and latex paint;

Vinegar, salt and citrus
   fruits.

Don't wrap or pack <u>plated</u>
<u>silver</u> in newspaper.
Printer's ink will, in time,
remove the plating.

●●●●●●●●●●●●●●●●●●●●●●●●●●

Camphor or alum in the
silver chest <u>prevents</u>
<u>tarnishing</u>.

Substitutes for copper and brass polish:

1. Slice of lemon with baking soda
2. Catsup
3. Salt and vinegar

There are more foolish
buyers than foolish sellers.

Anonymous

To <u>restore luster to pewter</u>,
try linseed oil and rotten-
stone.

●●●●●●●●●●●●●●●●●●●●●●●●

Stubborn <u>stains on pewter</u>
respond to mixture of mild
scouring powder and olive
oil.

Gently rub stubborn <u>stains</u> <u>on pewter</u> with fine steel wool.

●●●●●●●●●●●●●●●●●●●●●●●●●●●

Use black liquid shoe polish with its own applicator to <u>brighten wrought iron.</u> Does not rub or wash off.

Clean aluminum window frames
with silver polish.

Prevent aluminum doors,
screens, etc. from pitting
by wiping with cloth dipped
in kerosene twice a year.

Mineral or lemon oil rubbed on stainless steel surfaces will remove fingerprints. Use soft cloth and rub with the grain of the steel.

Culture is one thing
and varnish another.

R. W. Emerson

Brighten <u>chrome</u> fixtures
by rubbing with kerosene on
damp cloth.

● ●

To <u>remove calcium ring</u> from
toilet bowl, try pumice stone.

To <u>remove stains from Formica</u>
counters, make a paste of
baking soda and water; apply
to stain; leave on a minute
or two; rub to remove.
Won't scratch surface.

Clean Lucite terrarium with
rubbing alcohol, using a
very soft cloth. Will not
scratch.

●●●●●●●●●●●●●●●●●●●●●●●●

Use rubbing alcohol to
remove rings from stainless
steel pans.

To <u>clean ceramic tile,</u>
use vinegar on hard water
spots; kerosene on soap
scum.

●●●●●●●●●●●●●●●●●●●●●●●●●●

To <u>clean synthetic tile,</u>
rub with kerosene on a
damp cloth.

A human being: an ingenious
assembly of portable
plumbing.

Christopher Morley

<u>Substitutes for commercial products</u> designed to clean windows and mirrors include:

1. Borax and water;
2. Cornstarch and water (use with "squeegie");
3. Alcohol and water;
4. Ammonia and water.

<u>Windows will streak</u> if
washed when sun is direct-
ly on them.

●●●●●●●●●●●●●●●●●●●●●●●●●

Dry with newspaper or paper
towels for <u>lint-free windows.</u>

<u>Rub window</u> vertically
inside and horizontally
outside so any section of
glass that may have been
overlooked can be detected.

There is no better looking glass than an old friend.

M. Tupper

Solutions which act on
<u>alkaline deposits on</u>
<u>glass</u> include:

1. Lemon juice and water
2. Baking soda and water
3. Finely chopped raw potato
   and vinegar
4. Ammonia and water

⟶

5. Salt and vinegar

6. White vinegar and water

7. Grapefruit rind and water

Remove <u>tea or coffee stains</u>
from cups with solution of
vinegar and salt.

Never drink from your
finger bowl - it contains
only water.

Addison Mizner

To remove <u>film and spots left from dishwasher</u> detergent, add a little white vinegar to rinse cycle of the dishwasher.

Mix fine sand and de-
natured alcohol and swish
around inside of decanters
or vases to <u>make cloudy
glass sparkle.</u>

There is a crack in everything God has made.

R. W. Emerson

Place <u>cracked china</u> in
pan of milk and boil for
45 minutes; crack will
disappear and dish will
become stronger.

Glue pieces of old carpet or heavy wool to bottom of chair legs. This way the chair will slide more easily and won't leave <u>marks on vinyl floors</u>.

As slipcover is fitted to
your furniture, tuck rolled
newspaper into the sides
and back. This keeps the
slipcover tight.

To correct <u>sagging seats of cane chairs</u>, wash with hot water and dry in the sun.

●●●●●●●●●●●●●●●●●●●●●●●●●

Attach a large hook and eye to back of legs on <u>sectional furniture</u> in order to keep pieces from <u>slipping apart</u>.

Paint inside of wood drawers
in antique chests with
boiled linseed oil. This
helps to preserve the wood
so it won't split or shrink.

Home is the place where,

when you have to go there,

They have to take you in.

Robert Frost

When <u>stacked glasses
stick together</u>, put outer
glass in hot water. Fill
inside glass with ice.

●●●●●●●●●●●●●●●●●●●●●●●●

The <u>rims of crystal glasses</u>
are their weakest spot so
always wash or store upright.

Keep sprinkled clothes
in the freezer until ready
to iron. This does not harm
fabrics and makes ironing
quicker and easier.

● ●

"Iron" hair ribbons by
rubbing over hot light bulb.

When <u>covering the ironing board</u>, fit heavy duty aluminum under the regular cover. The reflected heat makes ironing go much faster.

Middle age is the time when a man is always thinking that in a week or two he will feel as good as ever.

Don Marquis

Tie small plastic bag filled with white vinegar over sluggish shower head and leave on for a few hours.

●●●●●●●●●●●●●●●●●●●●●●●●●

Cut sandpaper with scissors once or twice when scissors become dull.

Adding 1 cup white vinegar
to <u>final rinse cycle</u> will:

1. Keep lint off dark fabrics;
2. Soften woolens;
3. Keep plastic shower cur-
   tains pliable;
4. Prolong life of pantyhose
   and stockings.

Shampoo rubbed into soiled
<u>shirt collars</u> before
laundering helps <u>remove the
stain.</u> Shampoo is made to
dissolve body oils.

A little inflation is like
a little pregnancy - it
keeps growing.

Leon Henderson

Put 2 to 3 turkish towels in washing machine when laundering plastic shower curtain, foul weather gear, etc. The towels rub against the nonporous surface, help _remove mildew spots and dirt, and absorb excess water._

<u>Whiten nylon</u> curtains by
putting epsom salts in
the rinse water.

<u>Never soak rayon</u> material;
the fibers swell up and trap
dirt.

Rub <u>soiled spot</u> with
cleaning fluid and sprinkle
baby powder or cornstarch
on spot while it is wet.
.When dry, brush off powder.
No ring!

Remove "fuzz balls" from
sweaters with a dry sponge.

Protect zippers by closing
them before washing.

If <u>acid fluid is spilled</u>
on any fabric, immediately
neutralize acid action by
applying baking soda mixed
with water to the damaged
spot.

Familiarity breeds contempt--
and children.

Mark Twain

To clean oven:

Add 2 Tbsp. ammonia to pint of water; place in <u>oven</u> over night. Sponge off <u>grease</u> with warm water.

●●●●●●●●●●●●●●●●●●●●●●●●

Try baking soda to clean <u>glass oven door.</u>

Wear cotton gloves when
cleaning a chandelier.
Dip gloved fingers into
ammonia water and work
with both hands.

About the kitchen

Marbles in double boiler or
tea kettle will warn when
water has boiled away.

●●●●●●●●●●●●●●●●●●●●●●●●

To prevent scratching of
Teflon pans, place plastic
coffee can covers between
them when storing.

To aid in <u>cleaning</u> the inside <u>of badly burned pan</u>,
put outside of pan into cold
water while it is still very
hot.

Everything is funny as long
as it is happening to somebody else.

Will Rogers

To <u>remove paraffin easily</u>
from jams and jellies, place
a piece of string across
jars before sealing, letting
it hang an inch or two on
either side.

Dark deposits in kettles and
discolored aluminum or
enamel cookware may be
cleaned by adding 2 Tbsp.
cream of tartar to water
and boiling 5 minutes.

To <u>dry containers thoroughly</u> place a few sugar cubes in bottom after washing and drying to absorb moisture.

●●●●●●●●●●●●●●●●●●●●●●●●

To <u>remove jar lids</u>, slip a rubber band around lid and turn.

Use a pair of pliers to hold
<u>food to be grated.</u>   Food can
be grated down to almost
nothing.

● ●

Keep a brand new powder puff
in flour canister <u>for</u>
<u>dusting greased cake pan.</u>

To avoid spilling when
pouring liquid into a
narrow necked bottle,
pour it over a spoon handle
or rod inserted in opening.

Wear heavy rubber gloves to
<u>transfer turkey</u> from roast-
ing pan to platter.

<u>Darken the color of gravy</u>
(if out of commercial vari-
ety) with a small amount of
caramel or instant coffee.

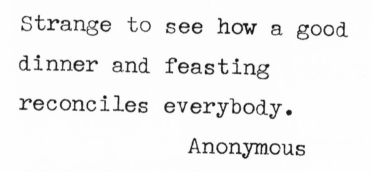

Strange to see how a good
dinner and feasting
reconciles everybody.

                    Anonymous

Truss turkey legs with
rolled gauze bandage.

●●●●●●●●●●●●●●●●●●●●●●●●

Do not put lye or drain
cleaning chemicals down
the garbage disposal.

Fruits and vegetables ripen
faster when placed in paper
bag or newspaper and stored
in drawer or closed cupboard.

●●●●●●●●●●●●●●●●●●●●●●●●●

Store poultry skewers in
plastic toothbrush con-
tainer.

Don't keep your coals in a volcano.

Publius Syrus

To <u>mince parsley easily</u>,
bunch the leafy tops to-
gether and cut with scissors
into a measuring cup. Then
to mince finer, put scissors
in the cup and snip away.

To <u>keep parsley fresh</u> for three weeks, place in a dry screw-top bottle and refrigerate.

●●●●●●●●●●●●●●●●●●●●●●●●●●

Put dry sponge in vegetable or crisper drawer of refrigerator <u>to absorb moisture.</u>

To <u>dry large quantities of lettuce or spinach</u>, put in pillow case, tie with twistie, place in washing machine and spin dry.

●●●●●●●●●●●●●●●●●●●●●●●

Use drying element of dish washer for a <u>heat drawer</u>.

Lettuce is like conversation;
it must be fresh and crisp,
so sparkling that you
scarcely notice the bitter
in it.

C. D. Warner

To <u>crisp celery</u>, place in a pan of cold water and add a slice of raw potato. Let stand for a few hours.

●●●●●●●●●●●●●●●●●●●●●●●●●

Use dental floss to <u>truss the turkey</u> for roasting.

There's somebody at every dinner party who eats all the celery.

Kin Hubbard

Keep <u>ready-to-use whipped cream</u> on hand. Whip 1 pint cream with 4 Tbsp. sugar. Drop in peaks on cookie sheet and freeze. Transfer to airtight container and store in freezer. Remove 15 minutes before serving.

<u>Keep rolls or toast hot</u>
longer by putting a piece of
foil under napkin in
serving basket.

●●●●●●●●●●●●●●●●●●●●●●●●●

<u>To re-heat rolls</u> put them
in a wet brown paper bag
and then in oven.

Light cream may be whipped
with ease by dropping one
egg white into it.

●●●●●●●●●●●●●●●●●●●●●●●●●●●●

To keep egg whites from
disintegrating while poach-
ing, put 1 tsp. vinegar in
water.

A small piece of <u>eggshell</u>
may be <u>removed from bowl</u> of
opened eggs by using the
half eggshell as a scoop,
which attracts the particle.

●●●●●●●●●●●●●●●●●●●●●●●●

To <u>avoid cracked boiled eggs</u>
pierce round end with a pin.

<u>Hard boiled eggs</u> will <u>peel</u> more easily if they are not quite fresh. Add salt to water and simmer 20 minutes. Plunge into cold water immediately.

A full belly makes a dull
brain.

                    B. Franklin

Egg yolks will keep up to
three days if they are
covered with cold water then
stored in refrigerator.

●●●●●●●●●●●●●●●●●●●●●●●●

Let egg whites warm to room
temperature before beating
for greater volume.

For fullest flavors in
<u>salad dressing</u>, mix season-
ing with vinegar before
adding the oil. Oil coats
herbs and traps the flavor.

What garlic is to salad,
insanity is to art.

Augustus Saint-Gaudens

When buying <u>tomatoes</u>, put
them in a paper bag rather
than plastic. While unload-
the groceries, put on a
kettle of water. Make a
cuff around top of bag and
put in corner of sink. Fill

→

it with boiling water. The
bag generally splits after
15 to 20 seconds. If it's a
better bag, give it a prod,
then, refrigerate tomatoes.
They're ready to skin.
Cherry tomatoes can be fixed
this way for marinating.

Rice will be <u>fluffier</u> and
drier if a slice of dry
bread is put on top of it
after cooking and draining.

●●●●●●●●●●●●●●●●●●●●●●●●●●●●

Season cole slaw, deviled
eggs, salad dressing, etc.
with <u>left-over pickle juice.</u>

<u>Broccoli</u> stems can be cooked in the same length of time as the flowers if you make X-like incisions from top to bottom through the stems.

"It's broccoli, dear."
"I say it's spinach,
and I say the hell with it."
G. B. White

Wash <u>strawberries</u> before re-
moving stems, to prevent
loss of juice.

●●●●●●●●●●●●●●●●●●●●●●●●●

Cover left over <u>olives</u> with
salad oil to preserve.

When a <u>small amount of lemon juice</u> is needed, don't cut fruit, just pierce with skewer and squeeze.
Refrigerate lemon.

●●●●●●●●●●●●●●●●●●●●●●●●●●

Add syrup to <u>pancake</u> batter for extra <u>flavor</u>.

Heavy <u>molasses or honey are</u>
<u>less apt to stick</u> if you dip
the measuring cup in hot
water before measuring.

●●●●●●●●●●●●●●●●●●●●●●●●●

Before <u>scalding milk</u>, rinse
pan in cold water to avoid
coating.

Milk the cow, but don't pull
off the udder.

Anonymous

To keep <u>cookies crisp</u>, place crushed tissue paper in bottom of cookie jar.

●●●●●●●●●●●●●●●●●●●●●●●●

<u>Sift flour</u> from bag to container so it will be ready to use in baking.

When <u>cooking tougher cuts of meat</u>, add a small amount of lemon juice or vinegar to the pot for tenderizing.

●●●●●●●●●●●●●●●●●●●●●●●●

Put <u>lemon on fish</u> after cooking, never before, to keep from getting mushy.

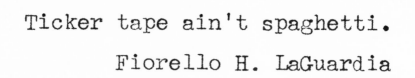

Ticker tape ain't spaghetti.

Fiorello H. LaGuardia

Canned <u>shrimp loses its
canned taste</u> by soaking in
2 Tbsp. of vinegar and 1 tsp.
of sherry for 15 minutes.

●●●●●●●●●●●●●●●●●●●●●●●●●

Thaw frozen fish in milk to
give <u>fresh-caught flavor.</u>
Drain before cooking.

Put a toothpick in <u>clove of</u> <u>garlic</u> to simplify retriev-
ing from marinade, stew, etc.

●●●●●●●●●●●●●●●●●●●●●●●●●●●

If <u>soups or stews are too</u>
<u>salty</u>, add a few slices of
potato. Boil a few minutes
and remove.

<u>Curdled hollandaise</u> sauce
can be corrected by mixing
one more egg yolk with a
little melted butter. Stir
into sauce, then add a
little hot water.

The best sauce is hunger.

Anonymous

To keep <u>brown sugar fresh</u>:

1. Add piece of fresh bread and close box securely.

2. Store in jar or clean coffee can with plastic lid. Add several marshmallows and close tightly.

3. Add apple, orange or

$\longrightarrow$

grapefruit slice; or add a
lemon peel.

● ●

Before peeling oranges,
cover with boiling water and
let stand 5 minutes. The
bitter white membrane can
be removed more easily.

Hollywood is a great place
if you're an orange.

Fred Allen

<u>Persimmons freeze</u> very well.
Keep them at room temperature until bright red and just beginning to soften.
Then wrap individually (and snugly) and freeze for steamed pudding or cookies.
Allow 45 minutes to thaw.

To <u>freeze avocados</u>, mash,
mix with 1 Tbsp. lemon juice
and 1 1/2 tsp. sugar for
each avocado. Keep com-
pletely protected from air
by packing in air tight
container and covering

→

with layer of mayonnaise.
Remove mayonnaise and any
discolored portions of
avocado when thawing.

●●●●●●●●●●●●●●●●●●●●●●●●●●●

<u>Nut meats</u> keep indefinitely
in freezer.

To <u>extract unbroken nut meats</u> easily, freeze at least 48 hours and crack while frozen.

Keep <u>popcorn</u> in your freezer for better popping.

True friends visit us in
prosperity only when invited,
but in adversity they come
without invitation.

                Theophrastus

For ease in <u>cutting meringue</u> <u>pies</u>, sprinkle a little granulated sugar over meringue before browning.

●●●●●●●●●●●●●●●●●●●●●●●●

To make <u>scrambled eggs</u> <u>fluffy</u>, add a little carbonated water.

Raw <u>mushrooms can be sliced</u>
evenly and quickly with an
egg slicer.

●●●●●●●●●●●●●●●●●●●●●●●●●●

To <u>cut fresh bread</u>, heat the
serrated knife.

For <u>even slices when cutting</u>
<u>bread</u>, salami, etc., keep
your eye on larger portion
when slicing.

●●●●●●●●●●●●●●●●●●●●●●●●

<u>Cheese</u> can be <u>sliced</u>
<u>thinner</u> with a dull knife.

In baiting a mouse-trap with
cheese, always leave room
for the mouse.

Saki

To help keep sliced, halved or mashed <u>avocado from turning brown</u>, refrigerate with its seed until served.

● ●

<u>Cream butter and sugar</u> together more quickly by adding a little hot milk.

To keep <u>mold off of cheese</u>:

1. Wipe cheese with vinegar.
2. Put 2 lumps of sugar in
   with cheese in airtight
   container.

●●●●●●●●●●●●●●●●●●●●●●●●●●

<u>Shave chocolate</u> with a
potato peeler.

A sugar cube in <u>olive oil</u>
keeps it <u>from becoming</u>
<u>rancid</u>.

<u>Bake potatoes</u> with a nail or
small skewer inserted to
shorten cooking time.

To stop <u>bacon and hamburger</u>
from <u>spattering</u>, sprinkle
salt in the cold frying pan
before cooking.

<u>Bacon</u>, when microwaved or
broiled, loses 9/10ths of
its calories.

The flavor of frying bacon
beats orange blossoms.

                    P. Benjamin

To <u>help eliminate odors,</u>
keep in refrigerator one
of the following:

1. Ground coffee

2. Vanilla

3. Charcoal

4. Baking soda

To eliminate <u>unpleasant</u>
<u>cooking odors</u>, simmer
vinegar on top of the stove.

●●●●●●●●●●●●●●●●●●●●●●●●●●●●

While cooking cauliflower,
avoid <u>odors</u> by adding a
slice of bread. It will
pour off with the water.

Strong odors can be removed
from fingers with:
1. Paste of dry mustard
2. Slice of lemon
3. Slice of raw potato

Fish and visitors smell
in three days.

B. Franklin

To keep "raising" dough from becoming crusty or dry, set a pan of boiling water and dough in unheated oven. Repeat while baking.

Let <u>dough rise</u> in plastic
bag; can be punched and
kneaded without drying out.

● ●

<u>Avoid soggy piecrust.</u> Rub
the bottom of an unbaked pie
shell generously with short-
ening. Then fill and bake.

Were we directed from Washington when to sow, and when to reap, we should soon want bread.

T. Jefferson

Put a bay leaf in flour and cereal canisters to <u>dis-courage weevils.</u>

●●●●●●●●●●●●●●●●●●●●●●●●●

Use a beer can opener to <u>remove stems from straw-berries.</u>

Date jars of <u>herbs</u> at the time of purchase. Some last only 4 to 6 months.

● ●

<u>Canned foods</u> lose nutrients if kept over a year.

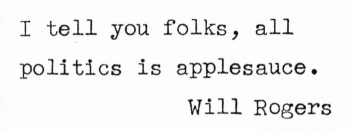

I tell you folks, all
politics is applesauce.

                Will Rogers

In the garden

Most <u>house plants</u> will produce astounding new growth if they get a daily "misting" of rain water or bottled water. An exception to this is hairy-leaved plants such as piggy-back.

Remember to fertilize all
<u>new house plants</u>. Grower
has fertilized for his growing period not the buyers.

●●●●●●●●●●●●●●●●●●●●●●●●●●

<u>Water house plants</u> with
water left from boiling eggs
or flat soda water.

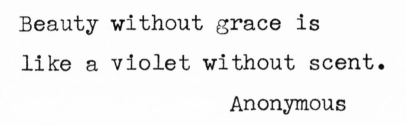

Beauty without grace is
like a violet without scent.

Anonymous

Support tall house plants
with an inexpensive adjust-
able brass curtain rod. It
grows with the plant.

● ●

Turn houseplants a quarter
every few days to keep them
growing straight.

Oil the saucers that hold
potted plants to <u>prevent</u>
<u>lime deposits</u>.

● ●

<u>Water hanging pots</u> inside
house by placing a few ice
cubes in pot. Melts slowly
and does not drip.

To keep <u>plants for a week</u>:

1.   Put a cotton cord in a
container of water which
is set a little higher than
the pot, bury other end in
the pot.

2.   Put a plastic bag over

the plants after watering.
Bag may need support from
a few sticks inserted into
the pot.

3. Fill bathtub with a
little water, place pots
on layers of folded paper
or on bricks in the tub.

An empty bag cannot stand
upright.

                    B. Franklin

To produce "moss" on new terra cotta <u>pots</u>, wipe with buttermilk. A growth of "moss" will appear in a few weeks.

●●●●●●●●●●●●●●●●●●●●●●●●

<u>Terra cotta pots</u> are <u>cooler</u> for root systems than synthetic pots.

Save your old kitchen sponges, cut into 1 inch squares, and use <u>to cover</u> the <u>drain hole in</u> your flower <u>pots</u>. Keeps soil in and slows down the drying out process.

Keep <u>soil from splashing</u> out of pots when watering, cover with 1/2 inch pea-gravel.

●●●●●●●●●●●●●●●●●●●●●●●●●●●

For <u>garden trash</u> wear an apron with big pockets or pin a bag to your belt.

<u>Keep planter from falling</u>
off porch or railing by
hammering a nail into the
wood and placing the hole of
the pot over the nail.

What a man needs in garden-
ing is a cast-iron back
with a hinge in it.

C. D. Warner

Hard coated <u>seeds</u> such as
sweet peas and morning
glory <u>start faster</u> if
soaked in water overnight.

● ●

<u>Discourage</u> <u>weeds</u> in cracks
by applying boiling salt
water, salt or motor oil.

To <u>store bulbs</u>, put them in empty egg cartons and label. They will be dry and un-broken for fall planting.

●●●●●●●●●●●●●●●●●●●●●●●●

For <u>gardeners' fingernails</u> clean with baking soda or twist fingers in lemon half.

<u>Mark</u> your <u>seed rows</u> by inserting empty seed packet into clear glass pop bottle and stick the bottle neck in the ground. Mark the packet with planting date.

Nobuddy ever fergits where
he buried a hatchet.

Kin Hubbard

Dip a wet string into pan
containing seeds to be
planted. The moist string
will pick up the <u>seeds</u>
evenly. Simply <u>plant</u> the
string and rows will be <u>even</u>
with no waste.

Plants that have been <u>frost bitten</u> should not be pruned until new growth appears.

●●●●●●●●●●●●●●●●●●●●●●●●●

Use an apple corer for <u>transplanting tiny plants</u> and weeding dichondra or other small plants.

A hole is nothing at all,
but you can break your neck
in it.

Austin O'Malley

Tea leaves and ashes from a wood fire make <u>excellent fertilizers</u>. Tea leaves also act as an insecticide. Used coffee grounds are good for geraniums.

<u>Protect</u> your <u>small garden
tools</u> from rusting by
pushing them into a pail of
oiled sand.

●●●●●●●●●●●●●●●●●●●●●●●●●●

Paint the handle of your hoe
every six inches for a <u>built
in ruler</u> for spacing plants.

A hedge between keeps

friendships green.

Anonymous

Change brand of <u>snail bait</u>
from time to time for
better effect.

● ●

Do not buy more than 6 to 8
weeks supply of <u>snail bait</u>.
Old bait is not effective.

Whenever I hear anyone talk of culture, I reach for my revolver.

Hermann Goering

Plant sunflower seeds to
attract birds away from
vegetable seedlings.

●●●●●●●●●●●●●●●●●●●●●●●●

Garlic and onion planted
in beds will help to
keep aphids away.

To <u>keep animals out of your</u> <u>garden</u>, sprinkle red pepper liberally or poke a few moth balls into the ground.

● ●

<u>Ants</u> do not like feverfew, so plant them near arti-chokes or vegetables.

A little Madness in the
Spring
is wholesome even for the
King.

Emily Dickinson

Daffodil and Narcissus
bulbs are toxic and they
help to keep gophers away.

●●●●●●●●●●●●●●●●●●●●●●●

Nasturtiums and Marigolds
help to control pests in
a vegetable garden.

Birds will use your <u>bird
bath</u> if you drop colored
marbles in the bottom.

To attract <u>humming birds</u> to
your garden, plant morning
glory, trumpet vine,
thistle or wild columbine.

The bird that flutters least

is longest on the wing.

William Cowper

For <u>longer lasting flower
arrangements</u>: pick materi-
als in the early morning or
late evening while stems are
inflated with moisture.
Cut stem at an angle to

increase the surface exposed to the water. Submerge up to flower heads in deep, lukewarm water, and put in cool dark place for several hours, or overnight.

Whatever a man's age, he
can reduce it several years
by putting a bright colored
flower in his buttonhole.

Mark Twain

When <u>conditioning greenery</u>,
a good rule to remember is
"the harder the stem, the
hotter the water". All
woody stem ends should be
split vertically 2 to 3
inches, so they can open and
take up water more readily.

$\longrightarrow$

Conditioning Flowers for Arrangements:

<u>Amaryllis</u>: Pick in bud stage. Add 1 Tbsp. ammonia to 2 quarts of water.

<u>Anemone</u>: Strip off some of lower stem. Add 1/2

cup of vinegar to 2 quarts
of water.

Aster: Add 1 tsp sugar to
1 quart of water.

Azalea: Crush or singe
stems. Use cold water.

California Poppy: Stems
or roots in cold water.

$\longrightarrow$

<u>Camellia</u>: Mist lightly
with cold water, insert
stems in a box of wet
cotton and refrigerate.
A little salt in the flower
center keeps it from
turning brown.

<u>Carnation</u>: Cut between joints. Recut under water. Condition in cold water up to flower heads.

<u>Chrysanthemum</u>: Defoliate as much as possible. Recut under water. Add 3 Tbsp. sugar to 1 quart of water.

$\longrightarrow$

<u>Daffodil</u>: Place in 3-4 inches cold water. Squeeze out milky substance.

<u>Dahlia</u>: Defoliate and immerse up to neck.

<u>Daisy or Marguerite</u>: Add 8 drops of peppermint to 1 quart of water.

<u>Delphinium</u>: Add 1 Tbsp. alcohol to 1 cup of water.

<u>Forget-Me-Not</u>: Use hot water, then cold. Cover heads with wax paper.

<u>Gardenia</u>: Split woody stems. Mist with cold water.

$\longrightarrow$

Geranium: Defoliate as much as possible.

Gladiolus: Cut 2 top buds from tip. Split stems.

Helleborus: (Christmas Rose) Crush stems. Add 5 drops of alcohol to 1 quart of water or use ice water.

Hyacinth: Split stem before placing in hot water, then cold water.

Hydrangea: Split stem ends, then singe. Add 1 Tbsp. vinegar to 1 quart of cold water.

Iris: Use cold water.

$\longrightarrow$

<u>Larkspur</u>: Add 1 tsp. sugar
to 1 quart of water.

<u>Lilac</u>: Defoliate except
leaf nearest head. Split
woody stems. Use cold water.

<u>Magnolia</u>: Cut in bud
stage and immerse to bud.

<u>Marigold</u>: Defoliate.
To avoid odor cut under
water with 1 tsp. pepper-
mint to 1 quart of water.
<u>Narcissus</u>: Use shallow
water.
<u>Nasturtium</u>: Pick before
fully opened. Split stems.

$\longrightarrow$

<u>Oleander</u>: Defoliate,
split stems and singe.

<u>Pansy</u>: Add 5 drops alcohol
to 1 pint of water.

<u>Peony</u>: Split stems ends
three inches. Defoliate.

<u>Poinsettia</u>: Singe stems.
Float in cold water.

<u>Poppy</u>: Singe stems imme-
diately. Use cold water.
<u>Queen-Annes-Lace</u>:
Immerse in cold water
almost to flower heads.
<u>Ranunculus</u>: Split stems.
Add 1/2 cup vinegar to
2 quarts of water.

$\longrightarrow$

<u>Rose</u>: Cut toward the last hours of daylight. Split stems. Add 5 drops alcohol to 2 quarts of water.

<u>Snapdragon</u>: Add 3 Tbsp. soda to 2 quarts of water

<u>Stock:</u> Split stems three
inches. Use very cold water.

<u>Sweet pea:</u> Boiling water,
then cold water.

<u>Tulip:</u> Boiling water,
then cold water.

<u>Zinnia:</u> Defoliate and
immerse in cold water.

Flowers are love's finest language.

E. W. Howe

Hold <u>long-stemmed</u> flowers
<u>erect</u> in a tall wide mouthed
vase by crisscrossing trans-
parent tape across the top.

●●●●●●●●●●●●●●●●●●●●●●●●●

A scouring pad of loose
plastic loops will make
a <u>frog for small vases.</u>

<u>Lengthen stems</u> for flower arrangements by inserting the short stems in plastic drinking straws. Trim as needed but be sure the covered stem reaches the water level.

A little inaccuracy

       sometimes saves tons

    of explanation.

                    Saki

For <u>difficult to arrange</u>
small stem flowers, place
1 inch sections of calla
lily stems in frog as a
tubular holder.

Place a piece of old stocking over a pin holder type frog when using it to hold oasis. When changing the arrangement lift the stocking to remove the oasis. <u>None of the oasis will remain in the holder.</u>

Put sand in a vase when the correct frog isn't avail-able and push flowers into wet sand. Also good for transporting flower arrangements.

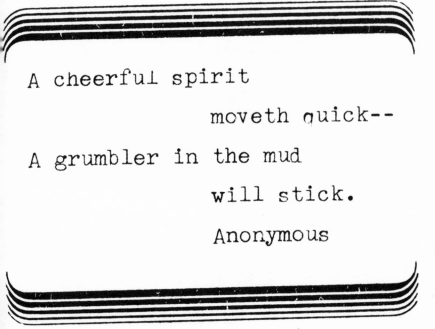

A cheerful spirit

        moveth quick--

A grumbler in the mud

        will stick.

      Anonymous

Drop a copper penny in the water with <u>tulips</u> and they will <u>stand erect</u> and not open wide.

●●●●●●●●●●●●●●●●●●●●●●●●●

<u>Rosebuds</u> will <u>open faster</u> if a lump of sugar is placed in the water.

To keep <u>water from clouding</u>
in a clear vase, add 1 Tbsp.
of liquid bleach to 1 quart
of water.

●●●●●●●●●●●●●●●●●●●●●●●●

A teaspoonful of sugar in a
vase of <u>marigolds</u> will help
eliminate <u>odor</u>.

Early to rise and early to
bed makes a male healthy and
wealthy and dead.

James Thurber

<u>To add</u> a sprig of fresh
<u>flowers to a fruit or vege-</u>
<u>table arrangement</u>, put a
little water in a toy
balloon, insert flower
stems and secure with
rubber band. Hide balloon
in arrangement.

Spray <u>dried flower arrange-</u>
<u>ments</u> with hair spray to
keep them from collecting
moisture and <u>falling apart.</u>

●●●●●●●●●●●●●●●●●●●●●●

To <u>freshen flower arrange-</u>
<u>ments</u> always add warm water
as it is "life giving".

Use a lazy susan to
rotate container while
arranging flowers.

● ●

A piece of charcoal in the
water of an arrangement
will keep it sweet.

What is the use of running
when we are not on the right
road?

Anonymous

<u>To make Potpourri</u>: Start
with 2 quarts of rose petals
dried carefully. Spread on
a cookie sheet and leave in
oven with pilot light on
for a day and a half, turning
several times. Put petals in

$\longrightarrow$

deep bowl and sprinkle with
salt. Cover container. At
end of a week add 2 ounces
allspice, a crushed cinnamon
stick, 1/2 ounce of whole
cloves. Cover for one
day and then add 10 ounces of

orris root, 2 ounces dry
lavender flowers or 3 drops
oil of lavender, 8 drops oil
of rose, a thin peeling of
an orange, and 4 ounces of
brandy. Mix gently and
store in tightly covered
jar.

When down in the mouth,
remember Jonah: he came
out all right.

Thomas A. Edison

All over the place

When <u>mailing cookies</u>, pack
them in popcorn to keep
them from crumbling.

●●●●●●●●●●●●●●●●●●●●●●●●

For large parties, use
washing machine to <u>store
ice, cool beer</u>, etc.

Freeze crystal <u>clear ice</u>
block for punch bowl by
using a mold and distilled
water. Add strawberries,
flowers or greenery if
desired.

When <u>cleaning</u> or handling
<u>freshly caught fish</u>, coat
hands with salt for easier
gripping.

●●●●●●●●●●●●●●●●●●●●●●●

Keep clear <u>plastic wrap</u> in
refrigerator to keep it
from <u>sticking</u> to itself.

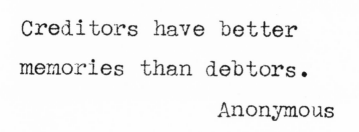

Creditors have better
memories than debtors.

Anonymous

Candles will <u>burn more</u>
<u>slowly</u> and evenly if
placed in freezer for an
hour or two before using.

●●●●●●●●●●●●●●●●●●●●●●●●●

Use dental floss <u>to mend</u>
<u>canvas or leather.</u>

Use a paper bag as a
<u>glove</u> when the <u>telephone</u>
<u>interrupts</u> action involving
gooey hands.

●●●●●●●●●●●●●●●●●●●●●●●●

Use a large plastic bag for
"hat" to <u>protect hair when</u>
<u>painting</u>.

Put an unwrapped bar of soap in suitcase to <u>eliminate</u> <u>musty odors</u>. Also effective in musty old drawers.

● ●

To avoid trouble at <u>customs</u> take along proof of purchase for new camera.

Custom meets us at the
cradle and leaves us only
at the tomb.

R. G. Ingersoll

Put paper towel on bottom of a travel kit to <u>absorb</u> <u>moisture</u>.

<u>To renew old broom</u>, dip it in a pail of boiling water with baking soda. Dry in the sun.

Silver weddings may have been, but more are forged of iron.

M. Tupper

<u>Sticky zippers</u> will slide easily if rubbed with a lead pencil.

●●●●●●●●●●●●●●●●●●●●●●●●●

Slip I.D. card inside window of <u>newly purchased car.</u> Positive way to claim car in case of theft.

Breathes there a man with
soul so tough
Who says two sexes aren't
enough?

Samuel Hoffenstein

<u>Cover the outdoor table set-</u>
<u>up</u> completely with colorful
nylon netting (72" wide and
little over $1 a yard) until
guests come to the table.
Food looks pretty through
netting and it's washable.

It is difficult to see why
lace should be so expensive;
it is mostly holes.

M. W. Little

Put the plastic lids of old coffee cans on the bottom of new cans to <u>prevent rust marks</u> on cupboard shelf.

●●●●●●●●●●●●●●●●●●●●●●●●

<u>Thermos</u> bottles lose <u>sour smell</u> when soaked in baking soda and water.

Wet string before tying
packages; as string dries,
it shrinks and <u>holds</u>
<u>package firmly</u> and safely
for mailing.

● ●

Hot vinegar removes freshly
<u>dried paint</u> on windows.

To remove broken light bulbs
without cutting fingers,
push large cork in broken
end and safely unscrew.

●●●●●●●●●●●●●●●●●●●●●●●●●

Unwrap bar soap to store.
It will harden and last
longer.

To <u>clean</u> a <u>sticky</u> deck of <u>cards</u>, put the cards in a paper bag with a tablespoon of talc or flour, and shake.

●●●●●●●●●●●●●●●●●●●●●●●●

To remove most <u>stains from suede shoes</u>, rub them with a piece of white bread.

Better that the feet slip
than the tongue.

Anonymous

To clean jewelry, soak in
ammonia, scrub with tooth
brush, rinse and polish with
paper towel.

●●●●●●●●●●●●●●●●●●●●●●●●

To clear a drain, pour in a
1/2 cup of salt followed by
boiling water.

The first thing to turn
green in the spring is
Christmas jewelry.

                    Kin Hubbard

To drive nails through a
board without splitting the
wood, insert the nail in a
bar of soap first.

● ●

A vegetable peeler is a
good substitute for a
Phillips screw driver.

An obedient wife commands
her husband.

Anonymous

<u>Tight or greasy screws</u>
may be <u>removed</u> easily
by applying a few drops
of peroxide. The bubbling
action will loosen them.

There was nothing more fun
than a man!

Dorothy Parker

To remove a glass stopper

from the neck of a bottle,
cover the entire stopper
with a mixture of 1/2 tsp.
alcohol, 1/4 tsp. glycer-
ine, 1/4 tsp. salt.
Soak for a few hours.
Tap and remove by lifting.

Claret is the liquor for
boys; port for men; but he
who aspires to be a hero
must drink brandy.

                    Samuel Johnson

To <u>revive old tennis balls</u>,
place in dryer for a few
minutes. Use warm cycle.

● ●

To <u>fluff articles stuffed</u>
<u>with down</u>, place in dryer
for one or two cycles set
at "warm" or "air".

When mounting pictures in
scrapbook, put <u>negative</u> be-
hind print <u>for safekeeping.</u>

<u>To preserve leather</u> bound
<u>books</u>, clean and dress with
warmed vaseline or lanolin.

All religions issue Bibles against Satan, and say the most injurious things against him, but we never hear his side.

Mark Twain

<u>To make original needlepoint</u>

<u>design</u>, take picture of

subject, have slide made,

and project on paper

mounted on wall. To adjust

size, move projector. Draw

or trace desired parts of

$\longrightarrow$

the projected picture
for the finished design.

●●●●●●●●●●●●●●●●●●●●●●●●●

To whiten tennis shoes,
sprinkle chlorinated
cleansing powder on shoes
while wet. Let stand.
Scrub, rinse, dry in sun.

Whenever I feel like
exercise, I lie down
until the feeling passes.

Robert M. Hutchins

272

To <u>preserve</u> a cherished
<u>newspaper clipping,</u>
dissolve a milk of mag-
nesia tablet in a quart
of club soda overnight.
Pour into a pan large
enough to accommodate the
flattened newspaper.

Soak newspaper one hour, remove and pat dry.

Estimated life: 200 years.

●●●●●●●●●●●●●●●●●●●●●●●●

To remove <u>ink stains from fingers</u>, rub fingers with a wet, unburned match.

A mule has neither pride
of ancestry nor hope of
posterity.

R. G. Ingersoll

To remove gum from hair try:
witch hazel, olive oil, egg
white, or peanut butter.

●●●●●●●●●●●●●●●●●●●●●●●●

To keep baskets from
drying out, clean with
solution of 40% castor
oil and 60% alcohol.

For <u>jellyfish and stingray bites</u>, use ammonia or urine.

●●●●●●●●●●●●●●●●●●●●●●●●

For a <u>toothache</u> apply piece of cotton saturated in ammonia. Bourbon, brandy or rum on the cotton tastes better.

Adam and Eve had many advan-
tages, but the principal one
was, that they escaped
teething.

                    Mark Twain

For <u>bee or wasp sting</u>, apply baking soda dampened with water or mud.

●●●●●●●●●●●●●●●●●●●●●●●●

<u>Itching</u> from insect bites and allergy rashes can be <u>relieved</u> by applying a paste of Monosodium Glutamate and water.

Treat <u>burns</u> immediately
by cooling burned area
with ice or anything
cold.

● ●

Rub mosquito bites with wet
soap to <u>stop itching</u>.

To <u>discourage fleas</u>, salt crevices of dog house, and wash the dog in salt water.

● ●

<u>To remove</u> skunk and other strong, <u>disagreeable odors from pets</u>, bathe in tomato juice or vinegar.

Where's the man could ease a
                heart
Like a satin gown?

                    Dorothy Parker

To remove lint from dark
fabrics, wind several strips
of scotch tape around
fingers and go over fabric
lightly.

To <u>keep moths away</u>, mix 2 handfuls each of dried lavender, rosemary, 1 Tbsp. crushed cloves and small pieces of dried lemon peel. Place in a gauze bag in dresser drawer.

Woman's virtue is man's
greatest invention.

Cornelia Otis Skinner

To <u>weatherproof wooden</u>
<u>matches</u>, roll them in wax.

● ●

To <u>prevent a door from</u>
<u>rattling</u>, stick a felt corn
pad to the door's lower
inside edge.

Before using <u>hands</u> in any <u>dirty project</u>, dig fingernails into a bar of soap. When finished, dirt and soap can be scrubbed out easily.

If you want to know how
old a woman is, ask
her sister-in-law.

E. W. Howe

Before painting, rub hand
lotion or vaseline liberally
on exposed skin <u>for protec-
tion, and easier removal
of paint.</u>

Approximate Conversions
to Metric Measures

Symbol	When You Know	Multiply by	To Find	Symbol
LENGTH				
in	inches	*2.5	centimeters	cm
ft	feet	30	centimeters	cm
yd	yards	0.9	meters	m
mi	miles	1.6	kilometers	km
AREA				
in^2	square inches	6.5	square centimeters	cm^2
ft^2	square feet	0.09	square meters	m^2
yd^2	square yards	0.8	square meters	m^2
mi^2	square miles	2.6	square kilometers	km^2
	acres	0.4	hectares	ha
MASS (weight)				
oz	ounces	28	grams	g
lb	pounds	0.45	kilograms	kg
	short tons (2000 lb)	0.9	tonnes	t
VOLUME				
tsp	teaspoons	5	milliliters	ml
Tbsp	tablespoons	15	milliliters	ml
fl oz	fluid ounces	30	milliliters	ml
c	cups	0.24	liters	l
pt	pints	0.47	liters	l
qt	quarts	0.95	liters	l
gal	gallons	3.8	liters	l
ft^3	cubic feet	0.03	cubic meters	m^3
yd^3	cubic yards	0.76	cubic meters	m^3

Approximate Conversions
from Metric Measures

Symbol	When You Know	Multiply by	To Find	Symbol
		LENGTH		
mm	millimeters	0.04	inches	in
cm	centimeters	0.4	inches	in
m	meters	3.3	feet	ft
m	meters	1.1	yards	yd
km	kilometers	0.6	miles	mi
		AREA		
cm^2	square centimeters	0.16	square inches	in^2
m^2	square meters	1.2	square yards	yd^2
km^2	square kilometers	0.4	square miles	mi^2
ha	hectares ($10,000 \text{ m}^2$)	2.5	acres	
		MASS (weight)		
g	grams	0.035	ounces	oz
kg	kilograms	2.2	pounds	lb
t	tonnes (1000 kg)	1.1	short tons	
		VOLUME		
ml	milliliters	0.03	fluid ounces	fl oz
l	liters	2.1	pints	pt
l	liters	1.06	quarts	qt
l	liters	0.26	gallons	gal
m^3	cubic meters	35	cubic feet	ft^3
m^3	cubic meters	1.3	cubic yards	yd^3
		TEMPERATURE (exact)		
°C	Celsius temperature	9/5 (then add 32)	Fahrenheit temperature	°F

Index

If you want to kill any idea in the world,
get a committee working on it.

                    C. F. Kettering

● ●

Co Chairmen: J. Wright, D. Hambleton
Committee:
          P. Foley, J. Jorgensen, E. Adams,
          H. Posthuma, F. Sheets
Design/Production: S. Kubly

All things bright and beautiful,
            All creatures great and small,
All things wise and wonderful
            The Lord God made them all.

Cecil Frances Alexander

If copies of

All Things Wise and Wonderful

are not available in local bookstores
or gift shops send inquiry to:

Pasadena Art Alliance
314 South Mentor Avenue
Pasadena, California 91106

and information will be forwarded to you.
Include your name, address and zip code.